Top Dog

by Cara Torrance
illustrated by Finn Dean

Kip sits on the mat.

Put on a pompom.

Kip can sip and sip.

Not a top dog!

Kip naps and naps.

No, not a top dog!

Kip can dig.

Not a top dog!

Kip can sit and sit.

Put on a pin!

Encourage students to use the pictures to retell the story.